*A Walk in the Woods*

# *A Walk in the Woods*

## Florence Turpin Morris

**VANTAGE PRESS**
New York

FIRST EDITION

All rights reserved, including the right of
reproduction in whole or in part in any form.

Copyright © 1992 by Florence Turpin Morris

Published by Vantage Press, Inc.
516 West 34th Street, New York, New York 10001

Manufactured in the United States of America
ISBN: 0-533-10139-5

Library of Congress Catalog Card No.: 91-91437

0 9 8 7 6 5 4 3 2 1

To the memory of my mother-in-law, Georgia Ann "Boggie" Morris, who lived in Franklin County, Arkansas, from about 1860 to 1935. She spent much of her life taking care of the sick or needy in her community. Her mode of travel was on foot, horseback, or horse and buggy. She carried in her basket croup medicine for children and many remedies that she made from herbs, roots, or bark.

# Contents

| | |
|---|---|
| Winter on the Farm | 1 |
| A Snow Storm | 2 |
| Snowbound | 3 |
| Skiing | 4 |
| Little Pussy Willow | 5 |
| The Groundhog | 6 |
| Little Brook | 7 |
| Spring Is Here | 8 |
| A Playhouse | 9 |
| Playing the Game | 10 |
| Little Tree Frog | 11 |
| Little Raindrops | 12 |
| Sounds of Summer | 13 |
| The Robin | 14 |
| Little Hummingbird | 15 |
| Little Measuring Worm | 16 |
| To a Head Louse | 17 |
| Meditations of a Baby Opossum | 18 |
| The Owl and the Chickadee | 19 |
| Welcome, Autumn | 20 |
| Halloween | 21 |
| Thanksgiving Day | 22 |
| The Snail | 23 |
| A Walk in the Woods | 24 |
| A Windy Day | 25 |
| My Inspiration | 26 |

| | |
|---|---|
| September 7, 1990, My Day | 27 |
| Valentine's Day | 28 |
| First Day of School | 29 |
| The One-Room School | 30 |
| A Teacher | 31 |
| Loyalty | 32 |
| Friendship | 33 |
| For Alan | 34 |
| Birthdays | 35 |
| A Bit of Heaven | 36 |
| Daffodil | 37 |
| Thoughts on Mother's Day | 38 |
| For Jeanne on Mother's Day | 39 |
| Christmas | 40 |
| New Year's | 41 |
| Forgiveness | 42 |
| All the World Is a Stage | 43 |
| Storm Clouds | 44 |
| A Wet, Rainy Day | 45 |
| When the Sun Sinks Low | 46 |
| Mourning Dove | 47 |
| Bunny Rabbit | 48 |
| To the Postman | 49 |
| The Rain Crow | 50 |
| Seashells | 51 |
| A Smile | 52 |

*A Walk in the Woods*

## Winter on the Farm

Through the night and into the day
The drifting snow blocked the pathway.
Near the shelter, where the animals waited to be fed,
The cow mooed safely in the shed.
While the pony waited in his stall,
Knowing he'd be fed first of all.
The "boss" with the loud voice
From the hen house started crowing.
Soon his importance began showing.
The concert soon reached full "swing,"
The best cackle was the thing,
Old "Shep" makes his rounds,
With leaps and bounds,
He is trying to say,
Everything is okay.
His only pay is a pat on the head,
Someone to care, some food, and a bed.

## A Snow Storm

Welcome, little snowbird, to my windowsill;
Stay as long as you will.
Snow covers the trees and roofs,
But horses have shoes that protect their hooves.

Through the night the snow flurries
Seem to bring no worries,
While under a snow-covered shed
Three baby kittens slumber in their bed.

While mother cat has gone hunting
For a treat for her hungry buntings.
I'm thankful for my post,
But what puzzles me most
Is how she keeps her feet from freezing.
But snowbirds and cats may have a secret
They don't share, or else—they don't care.

## Snowbound

When the snow had covered the ground,
The postman had made his round.
It was time for evening chores to begin;
The cows waited at the gate of the pen.

The sounds that could be heard
Were the twitters of the birds.
Soon the animals would all be fed
And go to bed.

The quiet old mare in the stall,
She never complains at all.
While the snow kept covering trees
And highways and byways.

Till the dawn, the snow piled in drifts,
As the snow plowmen worked in shifts.
The day ended with such fun—
A party was held for everyone.

## Skiing

It snowed all night,
Forests and fields, all wrapped in white;
A perfect day for fun and play.
Bundle up and buckle up tight.
Be sure you're ready for the first run,
A preliminary one.
The world is a wonderland of delight.

## Little Pussy Willow

Little pussy willow, I saw you sleeping,
But all the time you were keeping
Watch on the time of the year
For you to appear.

First of all
To greet your call
To the birds to wake up and sing,
The meadowlark brings the robin.
Soon all birdland is busy to see
Which builds the best nest,
Each doing its best.

The pussy willow's only reply
Was a quiet little sigh,
As if to say,
"I like it this way; it's been a beautiful day."

## The Groundhog

Little groundhog,
You're a harmless little creature,
But you have a bad feature.
When we want you to stay
In your hole all day,
You come out to play.

Now we know, and we're weary;
It's six more weeks that are dreary.

## Little Brook

Your pathway is always clear;
The message that I hear
Sounds like music to my ear,
As I gaze I wonder where you will end,
Or does your journey find you
A sudden bend?
After all, you have played a big part;
You've kept a clean life from the start.

## Spring Is Here

Said the robin to his friend,
"The message that I hear
Comes loud and clear:
Spring is here!"
The voice comes down from the mighty oak,
"Come build your nest;
My branches are the best."
Said the robin, "I've something to suggest.
The mockingbird will answer that request.
To sing at his best."
Said the oak with a gentle sigh,
"My reward is the song
And a long
Life of giving a peaceful home
To the birds."

## A Playhouse

The best place for a playhouse to be
Is under a big tree.
"Miz" Jones will live there;
The work is all done with much care.
First, a box will do for a chair.
The bed for the dolls can be
A cushion or a mat—
No argument about that.
For a table, a board on two rocks;
For chairs, just any kind of blocks.
Broken dishes are perfect for serving mud pies.
Give some to the doll that cries.

## Playing the Game

There's no better gift
To give you a lift
Than a wonderful day.
If you play it this way,
You can play the game and have fun.
Pick up the bat and make a home run.
Strike one! And you're on your way.
What a wonderful play!
You've made a score,
But there's much more.
You've decided to play.
What a wonderful day!

## Little Tree Frog

Little tree frog, I like your personality.
You're a perfect example of reality.
You're so cute,
But so mute.
I'd love to ask you what you eat.
Is it vegetable, plant, or meat?

You're so polite
When you show up in sight.
If you want to play,
You are welcome to stay.
When I found you on the door,
I wondered if you'd come to explore.

## Little Raindrops

Little raindrops on the walk,
How I wish that you could talk!
Thank you for the flowers that bloom;
They bring so much joy to chase away gloom.
Without the showers
There would be no flowers.
Thank you for the trees
That glow in the breeze;
For the animals that roam
In search of a home.
Birds that sing
Mean everything.
Come again
With a shower to bring.

## Sounds of Summer

Sounds of summer come loud and clear.
I listen and I hear.
The father bird sits near
The nest, and he sings
As he swings
For the babes who wait for food
The mother bird brings,
Never too late.

She works without complaining
All day long,
But gives thanks for the song.
His songs, without recording,
Are both welcome and rewarding.

## The Robin

Said the robin to a friend,
"The message that I hear
Comes loud and clear;
Spring is here!"
The voice comes from the mighty oak tree,
"Come build your nest;
My branches are the best
For safety from the storm
Or harm
That may come near.
My reward is your songs."

## Little Hummingbird

Little hummingbird, you've no song to sing;
But you've a message to bring.
We adore your magic wings
And marvel at other things.
You're a cheerful little creature,
But your most important feature's
You bring no harm to less capable creatures.
The dainty way you use your bill
Brings a thrill
At your skill
As you make the round
Till the best nectar is found.
You work with such might,
Bringing cheer and delight.
There's no time to tarry;
The food you must carry
To babes left in bed,
Waiting to be fed.
We welcome your attitude
As we are filled with gratitude.
Your visit's a treasure;
Thanks for the pleasure.

## Little Measuring Worm

Little measuring worm, you're so small;
Yet you have no spine at all.
Your mode of travel is so clever;
It seems that you never have any time to waste
Or any reason to make haste.
How important you are is not often told,
But you're from the days of old.
Perhaps your purpose is to supply a meal for a song bird,
To sing the best songs that we've heard.
You are perfect because God made you so.

## To a Head Louse

Said one young louse to another,
"Now that I'm through 'nitting,'
I'll go gadding about
Till my young ones come out."
The older and much bolder louse said,
"Take heed, this message you need.
That gun stands loaded, for sure,
The problem to cure."
They left in great haste,
No time to waste,
To start 'nitting' all over again.

## Meditations of a Baby Opossum

Such a strange place for us to meet,
Out here in the street.
Where is your mother,
Or are you out hunting another?
Someone to give you a home;
Or is it to satisfy your habit to roam?
You're so tiny, but so cute;
I wish you could talk, but you're mute.
I'll keep you if I find a friend
Who has a helping hand to lend,
And will find you a better place
To be safer than the street.
But no better friend I could ever meet
Out here in the street.

## The Owl and the Chickadee

On a limb of a dead old oak tree
Sat a wise old owl and a little chickadee.
They said to each other,
"There is no better place to be
Than this old oak tree."
Suddenly, below they heard a loud clatter.
The birds had all met for an important matter.
The crow read what the mayor had said,
"There's no good to be had
From a tree that is dead."
The woodpecker said,
"My little ones must be fed
From the worms that I get
From the roots of that old dead oak."
The next bird that spoke
Was the robin: "The bee that needs
Storage for honey has chosen that old dead oak;
So let's all agree
We must save that old tree."
The birds all took notes
To cast their votes
To save that dead old oak.
At the end of the session,
They made a confession:
"This old tree
Is worth more than money."

## Welcome, Autumn

Welcome, Autumn, come right in;
We've waited patiently for you to begin.
The wind plays a game with the leaves,
But we enjoy the breeze.

The fowl of the air that find new homes
For the winter
Have no worries about the renter.

The nuts begin to fall.
Kids come to gather them in bags,
Some big, some small.
There's plenty for all.
The animals get their share;
The chipmunk doesn't care.

## Halloween

A magic, big moon
Will be telling us soon
That witches will appear
Riding high in the sky
On brooms that can fly.
The moon makes the night
A season of delight.
Have fun, but beware;
It pays to take care.
Nothing is real.
Perhaps that is why
Witches ride brooms
Instead of wheels.

## Thanksgiving Day

Thanksgiving time is near;
It brings fond memories, but sometimes a tear.
But we must remember, all,
That we must do our part,
And give with all our heart
To feed and clothe the poor
Who may be near our door.
Some need only love;
All we share is from above.
For the feast we enjoy, we give thanks;
The turkey and the ham, right down to the shanks;
The pumpkin pies, all in a row,
And the baked potatoes, how fast they do go.
It's a day of remembering,
Forgiving, and for giving thanks
For the very first Thanksgiving.

## A Walk in the Woods

Deep in the woods I found
A most pleasant nook
Beside a little brook.
It seemed the birds were holding a concert
High up in the tall trees;
They brought joy with the breeze.

On the ground below
The raccoons put on a show,
Scratching the leaves in search of a meal
Or anything they might steal
From the squirrels or chipmunks.
The squirrels are never needy
Because they're so greedy.

## The Snail

From days of old
We're often told
That the snail is a slow creature.
But isn't there some other feature
That could describe this curious little critter?
It looks to me like he's a "sitter."

He carries his home on his back;
And wherever he goes he leaves
A little track.
If you're looking for beauty, or color,
It's not there.
He doesn't ask for care;
He moves at his own pace.
Has anyone ever heard of
A snail race?

## A Windy Day

Said the wind to the leaves one day,
"Come with me, I'll give you a ride in my shay."
Away went the wind, with its cargo held tight;
Over the meadows they flew with all their might.

The leaves found new places to rest;
The wind was happy that he had done his best.
What more can we say
For a windy day?

## My Inspiration

Christine,
When I walk into your room
There's never a sign of gloom.
Each time I stand beside your bed
And try to remember every word you've said;
And the smile that stays on your face
Gives me grace,
Courage, and hope
From a messenger of
Love.
As I walk away, I feel blessed from
Above.
"My cup runneth over"; I've found what I need.
Her life is written on her face
In word and in deed.

## September 7, 1990, My Day

It's nice to be ninety and alive,
But what about ninety-five?
Whatever is best,
I've been blest.
Each day is a gift,
And with it a lift.
To keep a good attitude,
And feel deep gratitude,
Remembering:
This is the day the Lord
Has made; Let us rejoice
And be glad in it.

## Valentine's Day

I'm feeling this way
Because it's Valentine's Day.
There's no better way
To say
What comes from the heart.
I'll look for words to convey
The feelings I'm confessing.
All the world looks much brighter,
And our problems seem lighter,
When a true friend can be near you
Or hear you.

## First Day of School

A tiny, little girl once started to school.
At home she had learned the first rule:
Mind the teacher, act nice;
Don't wait to be told twice.

She moved so quietly, she could scarcely be heard.
Her voice, like that of a bird.
With wide-open eyes, she showed no sign of weariness
At the end of the day.
I'll tell you the rest—
Her name was Fanny West.

## The One-Room School

There was no need for supervision on the playground.
No foul language went around.
Boys and girls played together.
We made our own rules that were fair to all;
The popular game was ball.
We made our own bat
From a board that was flat.
We made our ball from a sock;
Inside it we put a small rock.

The classroom was alive with competition;
Our goal was to excel in rendition.
We learned quite well
To read, write, and spell.
Arithmetic and writing
We took great pride in;
Spelling matches, ciphering matches were an extra treat;
As well as debates to see who beat.

## A Teacher

The friendship that I treasure
No way could I measure
Is a teacher named Akin,
Who did much in the makin'
Of many, many kids, whose skill
Would have become nil.
She told them they could be up with the best;
She provided the rest.
The admirers, far and near,
Love you and you know it,
But we want to show it.

## Loyalty

To Ed—
It comes to my mind
There's only one of your kind.
When you're needed, you're there,
With kindness and patience to spare.

It's hard to find words
To satisfy my urge.
The gratitude I feel,
I'm trying to reveal.
Forgive me for not saying enough that's just;
My effort is a trust.

## Friendship

A friendship that grows old
Is better than silver or gold.
When there seems no way to cope,
And you've almost lost hope,
You need someone to share,
And you know they'll be there
To comfort and care.
To rejoice when you're on the mountaintop;
And to stay close beside
When you're in the valley of despair.

## For Alan

The future ahead
Depends on how wisely you tread.
"To thine own self be true,"
Whatever it means to you.
To me, it means—to others, too.
If I've learned anything to recommend,
It's the most important choice of a lifetime friend,
One that's beside you in sunshine or in rain,
To share in joy or in pain.

## Birthdays

Birthdays are nice,
But if you think twice,
They all add up to years,
And almost bring tears.

A smile is a gift more precious than a word,
Or haven't you heard?
It works like a lovely song
To start a day pleasantly along.
It means,
Thank you, God, for letting me smile.

## A Bit of Heaven

A tiny angel lies asleep
In his bed
All wrapped in his blanket,
All warm and well fed.
No words can express
The feelings, better said.
Ten perfect fingers,
Tightly closed;
A soft little hand, so tempting to touch;
A glimpse of heaven is almost near.
Nothing on earth, so precious or dear
As a tiny baby, so helpless for care.

## Daffodil

On a hill far away
I heard a daffodil say,
"Spring is here to stay,
And now I must hurry
To tell the world not to worry,
But dress up and come out."

The crocus is everywhere,
Sending the word out loud;
And the whippoorwill sends a clear call
To large and small,
To be heard by all.
It's time to be happy
At work or at play.
God wants it that way.

## Thoughts on Mother's Day

There's a lot we can say
On Mother's Day.
But the thoughts we hold dearest
Are the ones that we cherish
When there's a babe to be fed
And tenderly put to bed.
And later we take a peep in,
To see if there is sleepin'
Or make sure we're finished.
We sit quietly to implore
To see if there's more.
We give thanks for a perfect day.

## For Jeanne on Mother's Day

I have this to say:
Somehow I just know,
As you watch Jack Ray grow,
He will have love to share
And kindness to spare.
By example you show
The best things to know.
What I'm saying is, May God's blessings and
His presence be near to guide you every step,
Every day.
What more should I say?

## Christmas

The story that never grows old
Is the sweetest story
That has ever been told,
Of the Christ child who was born
In a manger.

And there He lay
Until the break of day.
The shepherds watched their sheep
Not far away.

While Wise Men from afar
Were led by a star.
What joy they felt
When they behelt

The Babe!
They smiled
And worshiped Him.
The Christ child.

## New Year's

A new year is almost here;
We greet it with loud cheer,
Forgetting the cost, and yet
Many will have bills not met.
Just hoping the year ahead
Will help us to forget.

Always the glitter and glamour of the band
Will be there to take a stand.
While some will be praying,
Others will be saying,
"The world, full of sin,
Is the reason for the trouble we're in."

# Forgiveness

"To err is human,
to forgive divine."
We always remember
The first line,
But often we fail
To forgive or forget.
It's so simple
And yet—

Our minds hunger for peace.
This comes when we release
The ugly thoughts we keep
To keep us company when we sleep.
The goal we must seek to find
Is to forgive with all our mind.

## All the World Is a Stage

If all the world is a stage,
We begin on the first page.
Each of us has a different part to play.
Some are givers, not greedy;
Others are takers, always needy.

A smile is always worthwhile;
It's often returned with big pay;
And, always, it brightens the day.
It's not what we give, but what we share.
And with love, there's plenty to spare.

## Storm Clouds

I saw two fleecy clouds go by,
Floating high up in the sky.
I wondered as I watched;
They seemed to play.
When dark clouds are away,
I wondered why we, like they,
Couldn't have white clouds
Instead of gray.

But God knows best;
He gives the test.
Whether we have gray clouds or white,
We must remember
That nothing can happen that
He cannot handle.

## A Wet, Rainy Day

When clouds hide the sun
And you had work to be done,
If you start with a song
And stay cheerful all day long,
No worries can mount.
Soon you lose count
Of the hours that have been dreary.

Sometimes we forget that sorrow
Strikes others who need to borrow
A kind word and a smile.
A creepy, sleepy day is worthwhile.

## When the Sun Sinks Low

O wind! where do you go
When the sun sinks low?
We gaze at the magnificent array
Of colors at the close of day.

For a moment of silent meditation,
It's a moment of rededication.
Only the Supreme Power above
Could give this token of love.

A sigh from the gentle wind,
And a welcome breeze tells us
It's time for the birds to return to their nests
For a night of good rest.

God bless us at the close of day.

## Mourning Dove

On my walk through the woods one day,
I followed your call and found the way
To your nest and babies on a low limb of an apple tree.
What a treat was there for me to see!

The apple tree did more
Than bear fruit for me to enjoy.
It had given me the pleasure
I had never expected to treasure.

The sweet notes of good will
Linger with me still.

## Bunny Rabbit

I don't really see why
Some folks call you a bad guy
Because you stop for a treat
From the gardens on your way to greet
The dawn,
And watch the rising sun.
Think of the joy
You bring to each girl and boy!
At Easter time, the goodies to eat,
Baskets of treats.
You are welcome to come to my garden
As often as you can eat;
Or to rest.
I'll give you my best.

## To the Postman

Mister Postman, you're my friend.
You pick up the letters that I send.
You bring the letters that make me want to reply,
With a message of hope and that is the reason why
We should do our best,
And not worry about the rest.

You help old friends to keep in touch.
It's good to know that someone cares so much.
Thank you for coming in rain or in hail,
To bring us the mail.
When adversity pays us a call
We need letters to pick us up; we're so thankful for it all.

## The Rain Crow

I like to think of you as a whippoorwill,
Living on a nearby hill;
Bringing greetings of cheer,
And perhaps a message that rain is near.

But some folks call you a foe,
Because you steal their corn, row after row,
Before it begins to grow.
But your cheerful way will more than pay;
So you're welcome to come back any day.

## Seashells

Finding seashells is such fun;
Some are hidden, some lie glistening in the sun.
Some have been resting on the shore;
There're always plenty so you look for more.
Each one has a different story to tell;
And a lesson to teach as well.
Life has a purpose
We listen and learn
From "Life in a Shell."

## A Smile

A smile is a simple thing;
You smile and you hear the birds that always sing.
Before you know it
The whole world begins to show it.
To one whose burden is heavy,
A kind word or two can change a gray sky to blue.
Before the day is through
So many hearts are filled with gladness and cheer,
A feeling that kindness is dear.

It's a great, wide, wonderful world we live in,
If only we take the time to "give in."
A smile has a way of showing that you care;
What a blessing to share!